GW01375601

REMEMBER THE PARABLES

Published by CWR, Waverley Abbey House, Waverley Lane, Farnham, Surrey GU9 8EP.
Reprinted 2004.

See back of book for list of National Distributors.

Concept development, editing, design and production by CWR.

Illustrations: Jonathan Lee

Printed in England by Linney Print

ISBN: 1-85345-302-1

Remember the Lost Sheep

Written and illustrated by Jonathan Lee

The school day was finishing and the children gathered on the reading carpet. Mrs Phips had a special story to tell about a lost sheep and a kind shepherd. She cleared her throat, 'Uh hem', and began to read ...

There was once a happy shepherd with one hundred very happy sheep. Imagine one hundred sheep!

As the sun rose over the hill for a new day he counted his sheep one by one to make sure they were all still there ...
'One ... two ... three ...
SHEEP PEN HOTEL
NO VACANCIES
4
3
2
... ninety-eight ... ninety-nine ...
... ninety-nine ...'
SHEEP PEN HOTEL
NO
99
98

'... NINETY-NINE ...!'
Where was the missing sheep? The shepherd was now rather unhappy, and so too was the lost sheep.
SHEEP PEN HOTEL
VACANCIES
NO VACANCIES
24

The shepherd left the flock **straight** away and started looking for the lost **sheep**.

He looked up trees ...

... behind bushes ...

... down cliffs ...

... around streams. In fact almost everywhere.

The shepherd did not know where else to look, when all of a sudden he heard a faint echoing sound ... '... Bahh ... Bahh ...'

In a flash he picked up his crook and ran as fast as
his legs could carry him towards the sound ...

... And there in a cave was a cut, bruised, tired, hungry, and very thirsty lost sheep ...

... which now at last had been found.

The kind shepherd put the tired sheep on his shoulders and carried him back to the pasture to be with the other ninety-nine sheep.

There was great joy amongst the flock now that the lost sheep had been found. The shepherd and the sheep were now happy again.

99
100

Jesus tells us that God the Father is like the shepherd and the sheep like little children. He does not want any to be lost but all to believe in Him.

As soon as Mrs Phips had closed the book a little girl called Sarah put her hand up and asked, 'Why does God call us sheep?'

Mrs Phips chuckled a little, but realised what a good question it was. She thought carefully about her answer and said ...

'... Well Sarah, Jesus said that He is the Good Shepherd
who came to give His life for us, the flock.'

'We can only know God by believing in Jesus, God's only Son.'

'Like sheep we can sometimes wander away ... by not going to church, praying or reading the Bible.'

'Jesus wants us to belong to Him and not to wander away. Even if we do, He will always come looking for us, listening for the slightest bleat of a prayer, to carry us back to the flock. One thing is certain and that is Jesus will always, always ...'

'... remember the lost sheep.'

THE LOST SHEEP

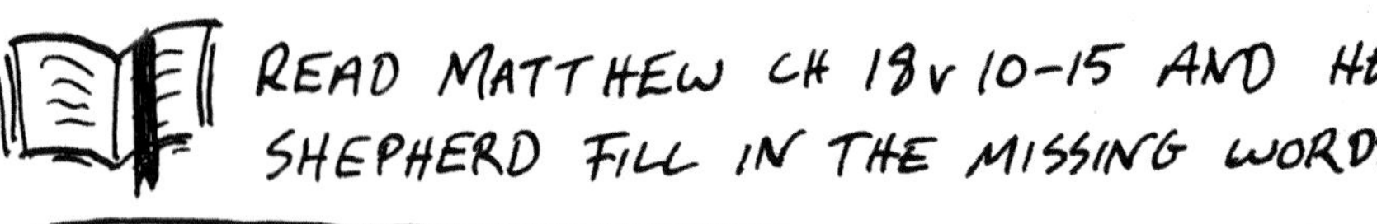

READ MATTHEW CH 18 v 10-15 AND HELP THE SHEPHERD FILL IN THE MISSING WORDS

JESUS SPEAKING OF CHILDREN

v10 'SEE THAT YOU DON'T ______ ANY OF THESE ______ ______. THEIR ______ IN ______, I TELL YOU, ARE ALWAYS IN THE PRESENCE OF MY ______ IN ______.'

JESUS SPEAKING OF THE LOST SHEEP

v13 'WHEN HE ______ IT, I TELL YOU, HE FEELS FAR ______ OVER THIS ONE ______ THAN OVER THE ______-______ THAT DID NOT GET ______. IN JUST THE SAME WAY YOUR ______ IN ______ DOES NOT WANT ANY OF THESE ______ ______ TO BE LOST.'

→ WE LEARN THAT JESUS IS LIKE A SHEPHERD AND CHILDREN ARE LIKE SHEEP.
WHERE ELSE IN THE BIBLE DO WE READ ABOUT JESUS THE SHEPHERD? → fill in the missing letters to find out...

PSALM 23 v1 T _ _ _ o _ _ _ _ _ y
_ _ _ _ _ _ _ _ ; _ _ _ v _
_ v _ _ y _ _ i _ _ _ _ _ e _ .

JOHN ch 10 v 11 'I _ _ _ h _ _ _ o _
_ h _ _ _ _ _ _ , _ h _ _ s _ _ l l _ _ _
_ _ _ _ e _ _ _ _ _ _ _ h _ _ _ .'

MEMORY VERSE Jesus says...

'My sheep listen to my voice;
I know them, and they follow me.'

John ch 10 v 27

COLOUR IN PAGES

Titles in this series

The Wise and Foolish Builders

ISBN: 1-85345-302-1

Remember the First Christmas

ISBN: 1-85345-317-X

£3.99
each (plus p&p)

The Good Samaritan

ISBN: 1-85345-301-3

Remember the First Easter

ISBN: 1-85345-330-7

National Distributors

UK: (and countries not listed below)
CWR, Waverley Abbey House, Waverley Lane, Farnham, Surrey GU9 8EP.
Tel: (01252) 784700 Outside UK (44) 1252 784700

AUSTRALIA: CMC Australasia, PO Box 519, Belmont, Victoria 3216.
Tel: (03) 5241 3288

CANADA: Cook Communications Ministries, PO Box 98, 55 Woodslee Avenue, Paris, Ontario.
Tel: 1800 263 2664

GHANA: Challenge Enterprises of Ghana, PO Box 5723, Accra.
Tel: (021) 222437/223249 Fax: (021) 226227

HONG KONG: Cross Communications Ltd, 1/F, 562A Nathan Road, Kowloon.
Tel: 2780 1188 Fax: 2770 6229

INDIA: Crystal Communications, 10-3-18/4/1, East Marredpalli, Secunderabad – 500026, Andhra Pradesh.
Tel/Fax: (040) 27737145

KENYA: Keswick Books and Gifts Ltd, PO Box 10242, Nairobi.
Tel: (02) 331692/226047 Fax: (02) 728557

MALAYSIA: Salvation Book Centre (M) Sdn Bhd, 23 Jalan SS 2/64,
47300 Petaling Jaya, Selangor.
Tel: (03) 78766411/78766797 Fax: (03) 78757066/78756360

NEW ZEALAND: CMC Australasia, PO Box 36015, Lower Hutt.
Tel: 0800 449 408 Fax: 0800 449 049

NIGERIA: FBFM, Helen Baugh House, 96 St Finbarr's College Road, Akoka, Lagos.
Tel: (01) 7747429/4700218/825775/827264

PHILIPPINES: OMF Literature Inc, 776 Boni Avenue, Mandaluyong City.
Tel: (02) 531 2183 Fax: (02) 531 1960

SINGAPORE: Armour Publishing Pte Ltd, Block 203A Henderson Road,
11–06 Henderson Industrial Park, Singapore 159546.
Tel: 6 276 9976 Fax: 6 276 7564

SOUTH AFRICA: Struik Christian Books, 80 MacKenzie Street,
PO Box 1144, Cape Town 8000.
Tel: (021) 462 4360 Fax: (021) 461 3612

SRI LANKA: Christombu Books, 27 Hospital Street, Colombo 1.
Tel: (01) 433142/328909

TANZANIA: CLC Christian Book Centre, PO Box 1384, Mkwepu Street, Dar es Salaam.
Tel/Fax (022) 2119439

USA: Cook Communications Ministries, PO Box 98, 55 Woodslee Avenue, Paris, Ontario, Canada.
Tel: 1800 263 2664

ZIMBABWE: Word of Life Books, Shop 4, Memorial Building,
35 S Machel Avenue, Harare.
Tel: (04) 781305 Fax: (04) 774739

For email addresses, visit the CWR website: www.cwr.org.uk

CWR is a registered charity – number 294387

I WAS LOST BUT JESUS FOUND ME

REMEMBER THE PARABLES